AF540961

A Woman UNPARALLELED

The Millennial's Guide to Create One's Self Worth

PREET SANDHU

Invincible Publishers

First published in India in 2018

ISBN: 978-93-88333-13-9

Invincible Publishers

G-120, Sushant Lok III, Sector 57, Gurgaon-122002

Registered Address: Opposite Kasturba Ashram, Radaur, Haryana–135133

Printed at Thomson Press (India) LTD

I want to dedicate this book to my late father.
I am thankful to Deep, Abhimanyu
as well as Manisha Chawla for being in my life.
Your encouragement pushed me to write this book.
I am thankful to Bidisha Bhuyan as you helped
me complete this book.

INTRODUCTION

"It is very important to know who you are. To make decisions. To show who you are."

~Malala Yousafzai

Every human being is born with one thing—the instinct to survive. It's not something that is taught consciously to a child over the years of his growth. The 'instinct to survive' is present equally in all of us, even before we assume an identity for ourselves. Let us take the example of a baby—babies are born helpless, in order to survive they are dependent on elders. It is the same with toddlers who survive by understanding the behavioural signs of their family members and other people around them.

For instance, my grandmother had a dangerous temper. Even in her eighties, she had the strength to take down my father. My behaviour was dependent on her and took form based on reading the signs whenever I was around her. Every individual is born with a habit to think about himself/herself first. This is an inseparable part of human nature. As a baby grows, his mental capacity grows too.

It is a well-known fact that any individual's contemporary situations and circumstances significantly affect his/her mental state and growth. Admittedly, it is not easy to have peace of mind when one is going through some tough times.

The fulfilment of basic needs will always be the first priority for any individual. Many famous psychologists and human behaviour professionals have described different categories of human needs. Only when all the basic needs—food, survival and shelter are accomplished—one reaches the level wherein one can think of living out one's inner passions, to find a place and earn respect in society, think of inner growth and contribute to the nation's growth, seek spiritual fulfilment, etc.

There are very few people in the world who know what to do with their passion. Sometimes, we have to keep our passion on hold, as it may not ensure our survival.

I am writing this book with the intention to lighten up the way for others on their journey. As a businesswoman, I have seen it myself and a lot of my co-workers have also gone through several phases in life and have done much learning and unlearning to reach where we were meant.

In this book, I have penned down all those experiences that I feel are significant for a person's growth through life, and it would bring me immense happiness if even a single thought from this book can contribute to bring even one per cent positivity in a reader's life.

My Journey

Through the course of my life, the one sure thing that I have realised is that I am a storyteller. Even as a child, I loved telling stories to my school friends, while today I tell them to my son and my colleagues. Here, I'd like to take the liberty to tell you that my stories have brought smiles to many faces!

Through this book, this storyteller would like to share her learning through various characters whom I have met during my journey—being a businesswoman and a first generation entrepreneur.

As per my understanding, story writing requires a deep understanding of experiences through life and its teachings. This is why I feel that no one can teach you better than a storyteller, who can make you go through all of life's learning and experiences.

In my life, one of the major factors that have played a vital role in deciding where I stand today are the decisions which I took at different points in my life. Without taking the decision of doing something or challenging oneself to do something, one cannot think of doing something worthy.

It has been eleven years since I started my journey as an entrepreneur after dropping out of my post-graduation. I knew one thing for sure that I wanted to create my own identity and flourish in my individuality, to stand out of the whole family with a badge of honour.

I wanted to make my father and myself proud.

With this thought in mind, I started the journey of my career. In those tough times, my strength and self-motivation were the only two elements of my personality that kept me going. I kept motivating myself to keep my aim high and create my own path to success.

An accidental wrong call from a consultant led me to meet my first employer in Chandigarh. We created a concept for an education industry together and started working on it accordingly. In no time, our business started growing and we received good success. Consequently, I realised that I could do something big with this man, and made up my mind to engage in business on a partnership basis. My aim was to create something big with my dreams.

Doing business also meant swimming in deep waters. Thus, I had to take several huge risks in my life and started doing things as they came my way. Today, my company is worth a hundred crore and the guy whom I entered into the business partnership with is now my husband. Sometimes when I sit back and recall, I have a hard time believing how brave I turned out to be at that time. With a startup company to manage, family pressures from behind and a new relationship, my plate was beyond full.

Today, with over more than ten years of experience in handling my own company, I feel I am eligible enough to share one of my best learning.

Taking the decision to start a business is a very courageous task, but once you are done with that decision and have made up your mind, be assured that you have crossed half the path to your success. Once you decide to form a business, you will come up with several ideas, and these ideas will provide you the inertia in your path towards success.

While reading this book, you will learn the three paths of life—the Identification Path, the Realization Path and the Implication Path. Through them, you will learn the following:

- How to identify your fears
- The factors responsible for those fears
- Decluttering the extra expenses that are not very important in your life
- How to be self-driven
- Saying No to a minimum of one hidden obligation, and speaking up against one thing, which you do not like
- Understanding the importance of hard times in life
- The very common traits of practicing to become a good leader
- How to maintain a healthy balance between your personal and professional life. This will be a lifetime success
- Incorporating confidence in your behaviour on a daily basis, and boosting yourself above the clouds to perform better in life
- Expressing your real emotions and always being yourself
- Investing in yourself, thereby creating self-worth. You are your own asset

- Reading a good book (In this book, you will find ways to find the right books that match perfectly with your personality)
- Learning a new language(s)
- Exploring new and futuristic technology
- Meeting good and intellectual people
- Joining online courses to enhance your knowledge base
- Maintaining your values that you have received from your family

Index

The Path of Identification

This path involves identifying the behavioural patterns that create or derail a conversation or engagement.

CHAPTER 1

FEAR AND ITS RESPONSIBLE FACTORS

Following this path by myself made me identify the following:

- Fears and the factors responsible for it
- Sources of positivity in the daily life incidents
- The power and impact of money and materialism

FEARS AND THE FACTORS

One of the best things about life is those small moments when you sit alone and find yourself reminiscing about old memories. Your mind space is entirely your own in those moments and the reality that you live through them is defined entirely by you. Once, after a long working day, I was sitting in my room, while my husband was away from town for work.

I have specially designed my room and customised it according to what I find best, as I like spending a lot of time there alone. It is beautifully decorated with a touch of old charm combined with the modern amenities, a complementing amalgamation of the best from both. For me, it is the most beautiful room in the house. My house otherwise is a hotpot of craziness for every passerby or stranger who doesn't know us personally, with the dogs barking, kids running around and making noise, and relatives laughing like there is no tomorrow.

That day, however, was the perfect day with the perfect environment for a person to go back in the past, walk down the memory lane and ponder over all the things that have been left behind. A memory in particular, which I have been stuck with since my childhood came to my mind that day. I don't remember the exact year, but I must be about ten years old at that time. The occasion was the annual function at my school. I had participated in an essay recitation for the event. My mother dressed me up in a beautiful dress, which she had bought especially for that day. All was well. I mean, I had practiced well and dressed up all pretty. What could possibly go wrong?

I was absolutely confident in myself. Everything was fine as I climbed up the stairs and onto the stage. All the lights were dimmed from the audience and a bright focus was created over me. This freaked me out. I felt the adrenaline coursing through my veins. My stomach dropped and I started feeling dizzy. That was the first time I had encountered stage fright first hand. Without any introduction, I started straight with the recitation and completed it in one breath as if I wanted to rid myself of the task and get it over with as quickly as possible. As I finished, I was glad and thanked God that I only had one essay to recite.

That evening, I ruminated over the various things, which used to scare me at some point in my life and tried to reach down to the factors behind them.

FEAR OF THE ALMIGHTY

As I sat recalling the strongest and deepest memories from my childhood, college days and the early days of my business, I realised that the one fear which had got deeply incorporated in me over this span of time was the fear of God.

In fact, the one thing, which has haunted me several times in my life, is my inability to engage in and continue my religious practices. This thought always used to bother me. Growing up, I was always taught to wake up early in the morning, go to the gurudwara to offer prayers, and read the holy book. As a child, I watched my mother practice all the traditional rites and rituals religiously, and of course repeatedly heard her say that if I didn't practice it, God would eventually stop listening to me. As a child, I followed whatever my mother dictated due to this fear of abandonment and retribution. It is not that I was not allowed to practice my religion after marriage, but since it took a lot of my time to adjust to the new environment, I could not continue it.

I am from Punjab, and unlike most Punjabi fathers who have a staunch patriarchal mindset; my father was a feminist through and through. He always encouraged me to pursue higher studies and believed that a big role in a girl's freedom is played by her economical independence. It was his dream to see me as a government official. However, destiny had other plans for me, and so, with its due call and partly mine, I completed my professional degree and started my own business in Gurugram.

CHANGES AFTER MARRIAGE

A big factor, which led to the birth of several other fears, was the fact that I had gotten married into a family outside my immediate culture. The thought takes me back to about four years ago when my son was only three years old. I was living with my in-laws several miles away from my parental home, and in a completely different state, culture and lifestyle. Being a Punjabi girl, I had seen a very open environment in my culture. Dupattas were not mandatory to wear over women's heads, girls went abroad for higher studies, daughters-in-law were not given the sole responsibility of taking care of the house, but went out to engage in work and business. Out here in Gurugram, however, due to a mixed culture, I felt a narrowness in people's vision regarding women, where the lady of the house is not allowed to pursue her dreams in her own way. Girls and daughters-in-law were not allowed to take any major decisions, and were not given much autonomy. They were still leading the kind of life which Punjabi women were leading in perhaps the 70s or 80s.

I took my jolly time to adjust to the mixed cultured society, the people, their way of life, mannerisms and code of discipline. At times, it made me wonder how in the olden days women who got married off to families in far off places spent their time when they were alone, or coped with all the changes that had suddenly entered their lives. We should consider ourselves lucky that now at least we have a number of distractions and indulgence opportunities to keep us occupied, like we can put the music system or the television on or call someone whenever we are not feeling that great.

My heart goes out to those women as I have walked a mile or two in their shoes too and have faced similar problems in my own life. Being married to a person who belongs to a different culture altogether also means that one has to live with and participate in two different cultures simultaneously, that is, one your own and other that your other half belongs to. This aspect of my life also fed my fear of God!

WHEN YOU ARE AWAY FROM HOME

Unlike most other girls in college, when I reached that age and phase of my life, I lived with the understanding that I had to come out of my comfort zone to move beyond one thing and get to the next. Despite the struggle still, my hope didn't die. I had always dreamt of doing something on my own, but with empty hands and deflated pockets, I couldn't think of starting something new. I left my studies mid-way and walked out of my hometown to work in Chandigarh, then progressed towards the next phase of my life and so on.

When I stayed away from my family for the first time, it was one of the biggest stepping-stones for me, and a major milestone for my life. I come from a very loving family with wonderful parents. Located in the suburbs of Amritsar city, my home reflected all the traditional characteristics. It is a big house in the countryside with six bedrooms, a beautiful garden out front, which is regularly maintained by my mother, and a play area where my father fixed a swing for me. This is where I had spent most of my childhood days. What I missed the most about my home when I moved out were the memories that I had come to associate with it. I missed having my morning tea together with dad and mom. Since we were a small family, we engaged in a lot of activities together, like going out shopping, spending a holiday out in the city, going out just to have a scoop of ice-cream, attending weddings, watching movies (I will never forget how much my dad enjoyed Sholay), etc. Though these were small activities, they were great source of happiness for me.

Every time I visit them even now, my home always reminds me of what an amazing childhood I had the privilege of having there. For this, I am truly thankful to my family.

Your parents are your biggest cushion that you can fall back on. Moving out of my house was like coming out of my biggest comfort zone to move forward in life. Moving out of Amritsar was the first solid initiative and difficult decision of my life.

STARTING A NEW BUSINESS

When I decided to leave my job and start a business, the same kind of dilemma presented itself in front of me in the form of a shaky predicament. I started my first business in partnership with my husband.

The vision for our new business was to become a bridge between industry and academia. We started gathering information on skilled manpower demands in the industry and shared them with educational institutes. We then started training the institutes to get their students placed according to the demand in the market.

When I started working on my first business concept, I adopted the method of converting an idea into scalable and profitable business model, though I had never read Steve Blank who popularised this idea in his writings. In 2010, there was hardly a startup craze in the market as it is today. In fact, with this concept, I got an opportunity in the market to meet eminent personalities and realized that they were giving lessons out of their old concepts/ theories and knowledge base. I have no right to prove them wrong, but I wanted to make them understand that a startup doesn't need systematic study of operations initially at the stage of research, particularly when one is only searching for a scalable and profitable business model. At his stage, one is meant to be ready to pivot and see failures–an integral part of any startup. It is very shocking but true that those very people did not encourage us to take the idea forward, but my husband was determined and unwavering in his intention to take it on.

My husband and I developed our concepts on paper, then converted them into proposals and started sending them to institutions. For a month, I continuously sent mails to institutions and introduced the concept to them. A few of them reverted back with just a thanks, while some called back to understand the concept better. Some even countered and tried to give me 'gyan' on how things should be, since I was the 'new kid in the market' for them. I was indeed a novice with little knowledge of the market standards and what solutions our target segment wanted for their problems.

My strength has always been that I am a good listener, so I listened to everyone but did what I wanted to do. After that crazy one-month of shooting mails, talking to people and doing all that I could in my capacity, we got a call from one of the good institutions of the state. My husband went and met those people. They liked the concept and gave us our first break. We organized some workshops and other activities, as mentioned in the proposal. We made good money in those days and got a break from two big government Universities immediately after this.

Institutions and universities started recognising the name of our organisation after a while. This is how we found our customers and crossed the first component of Customer Discovery of the Customer Development Process.

We did not focus on the product development process as much as on customers, and evolved over time as per the requirements. We did not invest huge money on the concept, but worked well on bootstrapping.

Back then, the social and professional environment was not so conducive to startups like it is today. With just one concept in our minds, we started our journey of entrepreneurship without any P&L visualisation, research, budget, or any professionally organised team. Today when I look back on our journey, I can proudly say that we successfully dealt with all the pressures and hurdles by adopting some simple basic formulas.

POSTPARTUM DEPRESSION

Every woman goes though certain tough phases in her life when she feels like giving up on everything. Such a time came for me too when I was struck by postpartum depression after the delivery of my child. I began to feel as if my life had gotten over, that I couldn't be the girl I once was. With a kid to take care of, I often felt that I may not be able to accomplish my dream of becoming a strong and independent woman again. Becoming a mother was a great feeling, but I was career oriented through and through. I started feeling as if the small baby was entirely dependent on me and that I wouldn't be able to leave him, and would need to put my priorities, career and dream on the backseat. A woman is most certain to go through this phase at some point in her life, and needs to come out of this depression on her own. I willed myself to get up and be back at office only thirty days after the delivery.

Those were few of the toughest days of my life. The closest that words can come to describe it is that it was like living in your own hell. Looking back, I wonder how I survived it and pulled myself out of it to eventually become the active and workaholic woman that I am today.

All these memories and instances from my life wherein I had to move forward by leaving my comfort zone have inspired me to write.

Coming out of this depression was like emerging out of a cocoon. At that time, I felt like I was reborn as another person, and I am proud to say that I fought all my battles alone.

This is another reason why I am writing this chapter. Not everyone's life is a bed of roses. This chapter is for all those lost souls who are searching for a ray of light to find their way onward.

Since I started writing, I started analysing situations more deeply and comprehensively. To those lost souls, I would say, try and figure out your talent, what you're good at. Art is a subversive tool that can help a lost soul express its guarded human desire, for art is the medium through which people can articulate their most profound and intimate thoughts, beliefs, expressions of love, desires and themselves unabashedly as they truly are. I not only express my feelings through art, but also leave a clue for future reference. At the same time, I am trying to convince myself to be happy and to enjoy every moment of my life as I go on. A realisation of this inner strength inspired me to write.

In order to achieve something, we need to override our fears. Today as I recall my journey, I can proudly say,

Left home, got a degree,

Left education, got a Job,

Left the job, got a business,

Stood up strong, got success.

Get up, don't just let it happen.

You've *got it (life) once*

So,

No excuses,

No regrets,

Fill it with fun.

Now when I look back at all those moments which terrified me, I wonder why was I even bothered in the least by such small and silly things.

As a child, various kinds of fears are ingrained into our psyche for various reasons in name of culture. Some common ones that we all have heard of are, *Do not go out alone in the night*, or *Do not travel alone*, and the list goes on. The first lesson that I learnt as I started the journey of my career was to unlearn all these fears.

Such fears are deeply embedded in all of us. This is why I am a huge advocate of self-discovery. Discovering oneself does not make a person centric, contrary to what many people believe. Rather, it helps shaping our mind in a way that enables us to live our lives with confidence.

It has also been observed that because of such fear factors, a major one being the fear of God and his retribution, our lives and actions and decisions get informed, defined and deeply influenced by them. We do things out of the fear that is deep-rooted within us and because we live in that fear, we are not able to listen carefully to our heart and mind. As a result, the peace and balance of our mind gets disturbed. Fears in mind always attract negativity.

On my path of realising things, this is the first step that I took, that is, to unlearn all the fears that I had by-hearted since my childhood.

The process comprises of two phases. The first phase requires you to identify your fears. This might take some time, more than you realise. After identifying each and every fear, start identifying the factors responsible for each fear. After identifying the factors responsible, find the best ways to eliminate those fears.

Let me give you an example: Stage fright can occur due to several factors like: I might look witless or stupid, forget my lines, be unprepared and gain the antagonism of the audience, and so on. The factor behind this fear is a lack of self-confidence. Some techniques that can used to cope with stage fright are: Practicing deep breathing before getting on stage, drinking a lot of water, healthy diet and exercise to keep your constitution fit, relaxation techniques, and last but not the least, practice! Practice on until you master it!

When I started identifying the factors responsible for my inner fears, I realised the real reasons that had been responsible for my distress and unhappiness too.

One of the best take on it is to just initiate action once towards what you want. Once you accomplish this, half the road to achieving your desires is automatically covered. It happened with me just the same. I identified the factors responsible for my internal fears, and this effort took me onwards on the path of becoming a strong human being.

TO PRACTICE

- Identify your fears
- Identify the factors responsible for those fears. If you are unable to identify the fears, just find the reasons behind your unhappiness

Make this book your personal journal and always keep it with you. As you read the book, you will find certain activities to practice after every chapter, which you'll need to work on in order to build a stronger personality.

CHAPTER 2

HANDLING NEGATIVITY IN DAILY LIFE

Since childhood, I have loved diving deep into every moment, living it in my mind after I have already lived it in reality and have always liked analysing different situations from different angles. Eventually, this became my habit. This might look as if I like overthinking, but I would like to share a small secret with you here. If you like writing, overthinking can actually turn out to be quite rewarding. This habit of mine has helped me a lot through writing.

I started testing my writing skills with quotes, which I placed on my office desk. I remember the first time I wrote down my thoughts on paper. I pinned them at my office desk. My colleagues in the office praised me for the words and it motivated me to think and write more like an actual writer.

Words have the power to change the world, unite or divide, make your dreams come true and help you express your inner feelings.

The practice of writing down my thoughts has affected me very positively. In fact, it has had such a huge impact in my life that I sometimes feel like I should start writing full-time and pivot my career towards it. I started staying up till late in the night to read more books and write more. As my business reached a stage where everything was automated, I decided to become a silent partner and act only as an advisor to guide the team.

Sometimes, we get thoughts like, ***Where am I going? What am I doing? Should I pivot midway my career?,*** and so on.

We all have to deal with some or the other form of negativity in our lives. The intensity may vary, but having to deal with it at some point is most definitely certain. Negativity leads to stagnation and creates unhappiness in life. As the famous Chinese philosophy of Yin and Yang professes, all contradictory forces like darkness and light, the positive and the negative are interconnected. The Yin and Yang symbol depicts the balance between the two opposites. Similarly, there must always be a balance between the negativity and positivity in our lives. It is very easy to fall into the negative trap of despair, which is why we must always keep our negative thought in control. Some easy ways to handle the negativity in our lives are:

- **Be aware**

  Keep your eyes and ears open. Find out what makes you happy, what makes you sad, what makes you curious, etc. The first step, which must be taken to release negativity, is to know your feelings and understand them.

- **Identify your wants and needs**

  It's amazing if you already know what you want and need in life. However, if you are stuck in defining for yourself what you want and need in life, you should follow this one simple step. Every time you are stuck with making a decision, ask yourself what you don't want. Don't ponder over it too much. As soon as you identify all the unwanted things, figure out what their opposites are. You will definitely observe a pattern thereafter, making it easier for you to identify and define things accordingly.

You won't believe the changes that I saw in my life as soon as I took this decision to start writing. I set up a routine, which I rigorously followed. I woke up at 6 AM every morning, exercised from 6:30 to 7:30 AM, went to office at 9 AM, returned home by 8 PM, ate my dinner by 9 PM, then started reading and writing for a good while before I went to sleep. Writing helped me explore a new passion, so I could not simply let go of it.

This passion made me feel alive and gave me the space to dream big on different lines.

Being a naturally curious person with a portfolio mindset, it is very hard for me to passively go with the flow of life, not having anything challenging me every now and then. Writing and making people like what I wrote was a challenge for me.

With my newfound passion, I engrossed myself into writing as much as I could. In fact, there was a time when I got ill because of insufficient sleep. Let me share with you an anecdote of one such incident, which took place on one such sleepless night when there was complete peace in and around the house.

It was late at night and everyone had slept. I sat on my bed to start writing. As I was struggling to write under the dim light of a tiny lamp by my bedside, my eyes wandered off to the darkness in the room. Still trying to write something, I got subconsciously absorbed into observing the darkness, and something came to my mind. I started analysing the importance of darkness itself, especially at night. A thought came into my mind as a realisation, that the beauty of night lies in its darkness. People like me are able to give time to their passions only in the peace of dark nights. I pondered over the beauty of night for a while and articulated this beauty as:

Night says,

I am tarnished

Since I am dispositioned

But in reality

I have my own beauty

And it accords

A very peaceful gravity.

This way, I started analysing my day-to-day experiences over time and began to recognise the positives out of everything. When I wrote, I was able to articulate all of it in my own words and thereby motivated myself to look forward to life in a very encouraging manner.

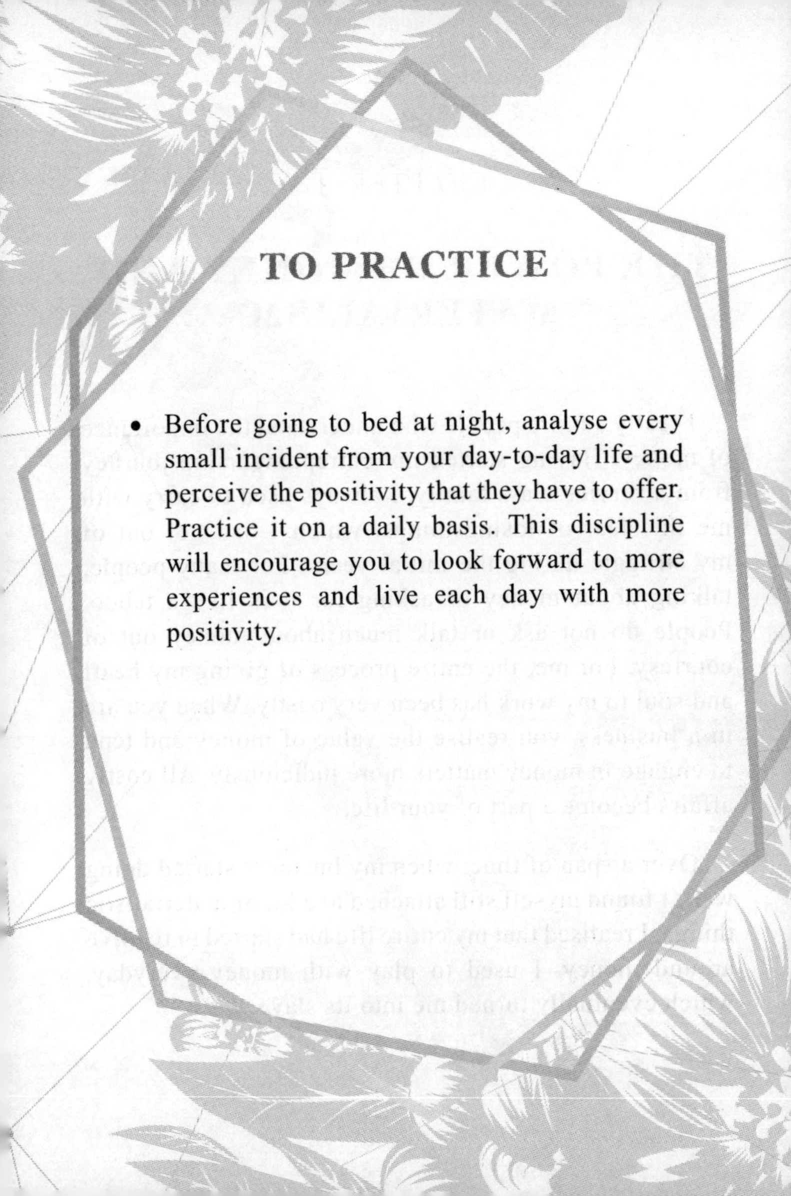

TO PRACTICE

- Before going to bed at night, analyse every small incident from your day-to-day life and perceive the positivity that they have to offer. Practice it on a daily basis. This discipline will encourage you to look forward to more experiences and live each day with more positivity.

CHAPTER 3

THE POWER OF MONEY AND MATERIALISM

I really admire people who understand the importance of money. Having started my entrepreneurship journey from a service class family, I always used to carry with me this fear of losing things, which I had got out of my struggle during the initial years. For many people, talking about money or asking for it is like a taboo. People do not ask or talk much about money out of courtesy. For me, the entire process of giving my heart and soul to my work has been very costly. When you are in a business, you realise the value of money and tend to engage in money matters more judiciously. All costly affairs become a part of your life.

Over a span of time, when my business started doing well, I found myself still attached to a lot of materialistic things. I realised that my entire life had started to revolve around money. I used to play with money everyday, which eventually turned me into its slave.

As ups and downs are always a part of any business, another fear that started hovering above my head was the loss of money that I had now grown used to.

This fear is sometimes so overwhelming and affected me so deeply that I could not envision my life beyond money, business and things at one point. This fear played a major role in creating several unhappy moments in my life.

One fortunate day, however, I got up early and sat down for a regular conversation with a close relative. We talked about several things, from attending parties to indulging in costly expenditures. In the middle of the conversation, he mentioned an observation that he had made of me. He said that I was not being able to comprehend the power of things, and that the power the materialistic things held over me was influencing me to become their slave.

While I agree that money is very important, if I had to think rationally, I figured that I should be avoiding all those things, which were turning me into their slave. I was setting off to my workplace and was on my way when this thought struck me that I should be avoiding all those things which were debilitating my rationality or were affecting my ability to make proper informed decisions.

That conversation with my relative that day actually made me realise that everything which is artificial actually takes away the genuine feelings of serenity from you.

To become content and happy in life, it is mandatory to realize the power of things.

Fear scares,

But fear says,

It is not me.

Nonetheless the power of things,

And you are the slave of power,

Once, the greed of power is finished,

I am conquered.

While I was happy with my life, having everything that I had ever dreamt of, there remained a void within me, which I did not know how to fill. I decided therefore to take the path of self-realisation. This path involved understanding my true self. My path of self-realisation involved the following phases:

- **Identification of my path:** When you start a new journey in life, the first thing that you must do is to recognise which path to adopt

- **Phase of realisation:** In this phase, one starts realising the factors, which are stopping oneself or hampering one's personality development. This is an ever-ending phase.

- **Spirituality:** On the path of realisation, when one starts disassociating oneself from the delusions of ego, the physical human body, etc., it means that one has successfully embarked upon the path of spirituality. In the words of Paramhansa Yogananda, '*Self-realization means realizing your true self as the great ocean of Spirit.*'

- **Finding a role model:** After understanding all my delusions, the next task was to find an inspirational role model or models.

- **Growth of personality:** Once your journey on the path of realization starts, and you attain spirituality and find a perfect role model for yourself, your personality starts improving and you start becoming very emotionally strong.

I am not asking for people to leave their houses and become a yogi, but I strongly believe that one can do something great for the society and the others by still being within the system.

Being a responsible human, it is always better to remain within the system. Leave all your fears behind.

By making our minds more powerful, we attain a magnetic and charismatic personality.

After going through all these different stages—Identification of your fears, Finding the inner beauty in things, rather than considering just their outer appearance, Realisation of inner strength and Realisation of the power of materialistic things, I started identifying ways to move away from all the unwanted things and cleanse myself of all the negativity. I started identifying and understanding the serenity in the natural form of things, like a simple evening near the plants on my terrace, or enjoying the peace in a room all to myself. As I started taking things as they came, I started realising the beauty of being content and at peace. I started realising the flow of time and started finding my inner peace with this flow.

This new found inner peace started creating a balance between my mind and my heart. My mind became more stable with due course of time. I found out that one's peace of mind doesn't exist in desires; it comes from being content.

To attain contentment or that feeling of fulfilment, I had to find a balance between my professional and personal life. You must be wondering how someone could stay away from materialistic things and money while in business. The answer to this question is one's

Emotional Quotient, which always helps one find different ways to see the same thing from different aspects and perspectives.

Emotional Quotient defines the ability of a person to guide his thinking or behaviour using the emotional intelligence information provided to him. So, sustaining with the truths of life and working as per the requirements of the materialistic universe is a real art which you will learn by the end of this book. Sustaining with things should be one of the most important elements of our everyday task list.

I have now reached a point where I am able to realize satisfaction and contentment. Now maintaining this state is another interesting part and a different chapter altogether.

Time is getting reformed,

Feel the content,

Leave the love for things,

Try once, this revolution is better,

And the best thing is,

It will also stabilise your mind!

TO PRACTICE

- Write down all the things, which you do daily, monthly, quarterly and yearly. Everything that involves you investing some money.
- Make two categories: One holds the expenses, which are absolutely necessary, like grocery, bills, etc. In the other category, list down all the things which are not entirely necessary, like nail extensions, spa, etc.

You will be surprised to know that half of your expenses can be skipped. You will realise that these things had only been a waste of your time, resources and money. Peace of mind can also be attained when you have some good savings in your bank account. Besides this, saving is a habit that has number of benefits.

Money is of course one of the most important factors for one's survival, but you must always be careful not to become its slave.

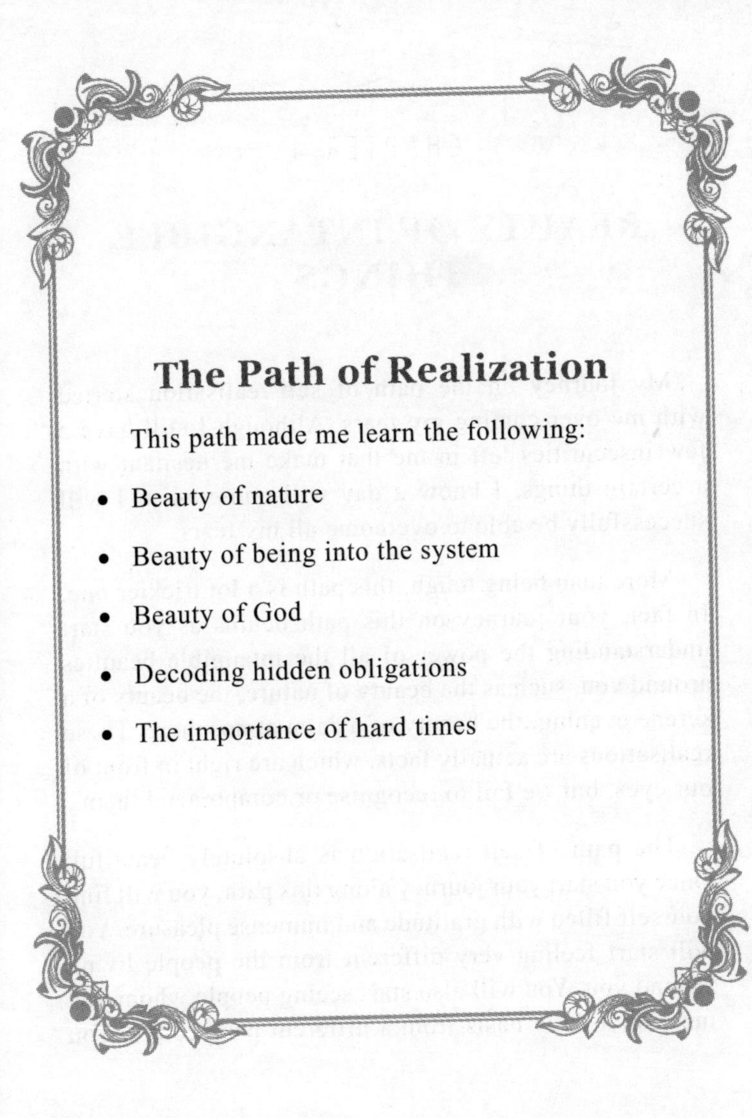

The Path of Realization

This path made me learn the following:

- Beauty of nature
- Beauty of being into the system
- Beauty of God
- Decoding hidden obligations
- The importance of hard times

CHAPTER 4

BEAUTY OF INTANGIBLE THINGS

My journey on the path of self-realisation started with me over coming my fears. Although I still have a few insecurities left in me that make me hesitant with a certain things, I know a day will come when I will successfully be able to overcome all my fears.

More than being tough, this path is a lot trickier one. In fact, your journey on this path begins as you start understanding the power of all the intangible beauties around you, such as the beauty of nature, the beauty of a serene evening, the beauty of a calm atmosphere. These realisations are actually facts, which are right in front of our eyes, but we fail to recognise or comprehend them.

The path of self-realisation is absolutely beautiful. Once you start your journey along this path, you will find yourself filled with gratitude and immense pleasure. You will start feeling very different from the people living around you. You will also start seeing people whom you meet on a daily basis from a different perspective. You will not only gain more knowledge, but also become wiser.

As I started off on this path, I began analysing every single thing in my daily life very deeply. While I was analysing every action as well as reaction of the people involved with me in my life daily, a major issue came to the surface and registered in my mind. I would like to bring it to the notice of all who are reading this. This is a problem that we face not only in our professional lives, but also in our personal lives. Let's start with a simple question—How many of you know people or have friends who have a reactionary nature?

We have all met at least one such person in our lives. Reactive people are defined as those who only react, that is, they only act in response to the others. Such an attitude does not only affect the one person on the receiving end, but the entire work culture. Reactive people, with all due respect to their emotions, have the ability to not only destroy a business, but also relationships. They are ticking time bombs, which can explode at any moment.

In order to ensure pro-activeness in life, the following steps must be taken:

- **Learn new skills**

This must be kept as the first priority. No matter how busy you are or how tight your schedule is, you must always take out some time from your day to learn new skills.

- **Don't just work or wait for the orders**

Rather, find out ways to improve your own work.

- **Plan**

Don't waste time and wait for the last minute to complete any work. Rather, plan your work and try to complete it beforehand.

- **Emphasise on values, rather than feelings**

Reactive people take things very seriously. For example, if somebody has commented on them regarding something, they will keep thinking about it for the entire day. Proactive people, on the other hand, act differently and consider such comments as only their opinions, and leave it at that.

- **Take responsibility**

Reactive people blame others, while proactive people take responsibility and make sure that they do not make the same mistakes again. They think about their own interest; they only want to get their work done, and that is the only purpose they strive to serve the whole day.

This journey, however, helped me change this viewpoint.

As it had become my habit to observe people deeply on a daily basis, I started feeling that the opinion I held for them was actually negative. It was me, not them. I realised that just because their core values are different from mine, it does not necessarily mean that they are evil or selfish. Everyone has the right to be however they are. As long as their actions or words did not hurt anyone, it hardly mattered.

These observation habits led me to understand the beauty of being in the system and realise the deep knowledge of the temporary situations of life. One of the biggest things I learnt while walking this path was that walking away from any situation is very easy, but as Rama Krishna said, 'One gets everything done only when one does the things by being in the system'.

What he meant was that life happens only when you remain in the system. When you are out of the system, you simply wait for your life to get over and see it passing by every single day. I remained in the system. Due to such realisations, I was able to understand what people were expecting out of me. I made decisions based on the way it satisfied me, and made sure that I completed the purpose of my life.

In fact, I would like to thank each of that person who put me through a tough situation, because it was those situations that made me learn how to take decisions in life by balancing everyone and everything.

The path of realisation also made me learn the difference between God and religion. This truth will help you understand the logic behind the religious practices that we follow on a daily basis too. Both these realisations made me reinterpret some of the biggest incidents of my life, which eventually made me a writer and a speaker. My family and my son wanted me to be at home on time everyday. Here, my values played a big role and encouraged me to identify the way out to reach people and the youth. I wanted to do it, but by remaining within the system.

People are scared of you (GOD),

An illogical fear for the most adoring and beautiful creator of the Universe,

To conquer their anxiety, they follow customs blindly without understanding their rationalities,

Where as the fact is,

For ages, spirituality is being confused for the fear of GOD.

Meditation is a tool to enhance our spiritual growth,

It helps us embrace our worries, our anger, and our fears

It heals and helps stabilise our emotions,

Reading the holy books is another important tool to surge up our wisdom.

It gives us power to focus on the purpose of life,

Gives power to identify the path to accomplish it,

Helps rectify the difficult situations of life,

Hence, meditation and reading holy books gives spiritual guidance to the one who follows it consistently,

It is phenomenal when one experiences such guidance,

And I am lucky enough to have got that,

I have to focus on my dreams,

Have to work to accomplish my vision,

Have to explore my talents and potential,

But not at the cost of significant relations,

They are doing everything for my happiness,

Their love is increasing over the span of time,

Their disapproval should be considered and taken care of,

That is the only way out to balance life and dreams.

The horizon of your thought process starts widening and you start going with the flow of life. You become more patient, you start recognising the importance of work in your life. In fact, the importance of a positive aura and a positive thought process is understood very well too. A lot of changes take place during this process, which also has the power to turn you into a saint. As Dr Joseph Murphy has explained well in his book *The Power of Your Subconscious Mind* that there are two types of minds—The Magnetised Mind, and the Un-magnetised Mind. The former is a powerful mind, which always visualises the positivity in every activity and takes on the risk to work on it, while the latter is always full of fear, always thinking of the risk of destroying the existing things. An Un-magnetised mind does not allow a person to move forward to explore new things. That is why they always remain on the same stage of life. They are not able to upgrade their living standards or networking or social life.

At this stage, I could recognise that both my conscious and subconscious minds had to be free of the shackles of fear and anxiety. For this, I had started reading more and more books to release my mind from the slavery of things, and to fall for the beauty of nature.

This is a small glimpse of how I felt about the beauty of nature and a serene evening:

A sunny midwinter afternoon,

A scenic terrace, full of plants & pots,

A lovely grass carpet alongside the plants,

An open sky, top floor, no one around,

A mug of hot coffee,

A soft pillow,

Relaxed mood,

A favourite light music on,

Is

A unique way to experience the tranquility of the moment.

Oh, God! This world is a divine craft.

Few words to the beautiful evening,

Beautiful you are,

Calm you are,

Serene you are,

Striking you are,

I Love your tranquility,

Feel like leaning in you,

Hey! Peaceful moment! Engulf me within you forever.

Beauty is everywhere, one just needs to find it. Beauty is not just in nature, but also in people. Once you start looking into the factors, which make people beautiful, you will start seeing them in everyone, and you will start finding everyone beautiful. Life is more than grief, sorrow and anger. It is also about happiness, love and beauty. Life can be tough sometimes, just to challenge you. No matter how hard life comes on you, never think that you are insignificant. All contradictory forces like light-dark, male-female, good-bad are important to sustain life.

What image comes to your mind when you think of beauty? Do you see images of people, mountains, trees, forest, etc.? Beauty is, in fact, everywhere. You just have to let yourself feel it. Go out for an adventure, meet new people, listen to the stories that people have to say. Love with all your heart and find the beauty in yourself and the universe.

TO PRACTICE

- Write down the positive and the negative traits of people whom you meet on a daily basis. Try to focus on their positive traits and start incorporating the positive ones in yourself.
- If your dreams and responsibilities require you to be into the system (like a relationship, a job, a partnership and many more likewise), start realising the situations and things which encourage you to move out of the system.
- Post writing, start finding the possible ways out to fight with the situation.

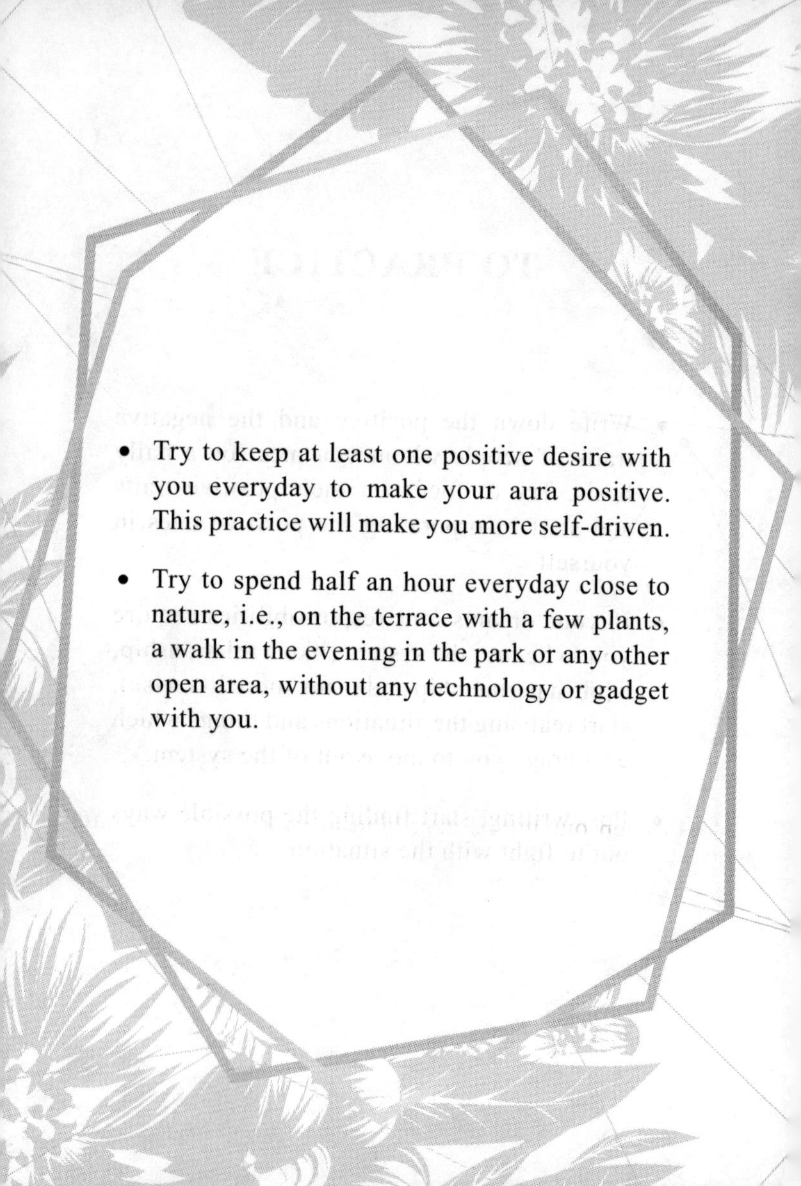

- Try to keep at least one positive desire with you everyday to make your aura positive. This practice will make you more self-driven.
- Try to spend half an hour everyday close to nature, i.e., on the terrace with a few plants, a walk in the evening in the park or any other open area, without any technology or gadget with you.

CHAPTER 5

DECODING THE HIDDEN OBLIGATIONS

Sometimes, we do a lot of things to please others; we oblige for their happiness. When our lives start depending on others, or are based on others' decisions, it proves that we are living our lives to please the society, the people and our relationships. This is one main reason why most people get frustrated so easily these days. We blindly follow the path shown to us by the society, but the truth is that the only path we should be following is the path shown to us by our own heart.

To deal with frustration in our daily lives, we must remove or deduct everything, which is toxic in our lives, and keep our minds calm and at peace. Understanding and being aware of all the toxic things is also a kind of realization which will lead you on to another path where you will start thinking about what makes you feel satisfied and happy, and what keeps you in a calm state of mind.

If you want to grow in life and wish to achieve something, you'll need to de-clutter all those actions and routines, which you do to please others. You'll need to start becoming a very transparent and clear person.

- Learn to say No to those things, which you can't do by taking ownership. It is the best practice to de-clutter all the unnecessary things from life.

- Don't soak things in, either ignore them or speak up. This is the best practice to make you strong enough on a daily basis.

Doing things doesn't hurt,

But

Doing it to oblige others, always

Hurts

Hardly matters

Either obligation is

To stay in a relationship

Or

To keep it safe.

It is not very easy to recognise all the hidden obligations which you follow on a daily basis; this needs practice. Once you are able to do that, you will easily be able to do it on a daily basis. It took me no less than five years to identify the hidden obligations in my life. Being very career oriented from the start, and now a newly married lady, it was getting increasingly difficult for me to handle both the personal and professional sides of my life. Most times, I have seen that we are not able to maintain a balance between our personal and professional life.

It becomes difficult for us to handle everything due to a common reason that we don't know 'How to say No and speak up to express opinion regarding the non-viable things'. We start every day with complaints, then dealt with the pressures of the workplace, then regretted at night for not having given complete time and attention to family and children. It is the case with every married millennial lady. Over a span of time, when I was on the path of realizing and observing my own life, I decoded all the obligations and started to de-clutter all the unnecessary things out of my life.

TO PRACTICE

- Write down the tasks, which you do on a daily basis to please others. Here, I would like to point out the difference between responsibilities and obligations. For instance, working for the treatment of your family member is not an obligation, but a responsibility, but working overtime in your office to please your boss is an obligation.
- On a daily a basis, start saying No to at least one hidden obligation and speak up for one thing which you do not like.

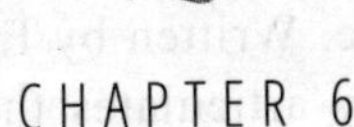

CHAPTER 6

THE IMPORTANCE OF HARD TIMES

It isn't about what we have missed,

What is to be merited is not in our grasp

What we long for, we ought to have...

As we move on in life, we outgrow the things or people who used to be important to us at some point of our lives or another. There is nothing wrong with it. We outgrow them because our priorities change with time, our inclinations take a different turn and our passion takes new forms.

Remember, if you are aggressively passionate about something, then you are made for it!

We all have faced some hurdle or another in our lives. These tough times are important, as they not only make you strong, but also define your personality. At this point, a poem comes to my mind. I have fallen in love with it ever since I laid my eyes on it. It has never failed to motivate me, especially when I have had to go through a tough time. Written by Ella Wheeler Wilcox, the poem beautifully articulates the positive aspect of solitude and being alone.

Laugh, and the world laughs with you;

Weep, and you weep alone;

For the sad old earth must borrow its mirth,

But has trouble enough of its own.

Sing, and the hills will answer;

Sigh, it is lost on the air;

The echoes bound to a joyful sound,

But shrink from voicing care.

Rejoice, and men will seek you;

Grieve, and they turn and go;

They want full measure of all your pleasure,

But they do not need your woe.

Be glad, and your friends are many;

Be sad, and you lose them all,—

There are none to decline your nectared wine,

But alone you must drink life's gall.

Feast, and your halls are crowded;

Fast, and the world goes by.

Succeed and give, and it helps you live,

But no man can help you die.

There is room in the halls of pleasure

For a large and lordly train,

But one by one we must all file on

Through the narrow aisles of pain.

The most difficult time for me started when I decided to start my entrepreneurship journey, even though I knew that it was too hard as a career to choose. In those days, particularly, even the environment was not encouraging for startups.

My hardships started when I got a call from a consultant with the offer to join a startup company. I started off as an employee, but ended up becoming a partner. This was the best phase of my life. Starting a new business was not that easy in those times. Unlike today, there were very few active investors in those days. Furthermore, startups were not encouraged at that time.

If I had to divide the experience of my business life, I would divide it into four phases. In the first phase, we thought of a concept and tried it in the market. Even though our concept invited huge attraction, the curve eventually declined because of the lack of money, and as there was such a business model around it. So, they finally decided to shut it down.

Sometimes by losing a battle, you find a new way to win the war.

This is exactly what happened next. Due to the lack of professional help and knowledge, we could not continue with our first business. The second phase started when I joined another job after some time. During this process, I met several people, including the CHROs (Chief Human Resource Officers), HR experts, mentors, etc. This job actually helped me understand the various faults that we had made with our first startup. After gaining a few years of experience in that industry, I learnt various skills.

The third phase of our business started when I decided to back to my business again. This time, I had good experience and skills on my hand, which helped me keep the business stable.

Just like an individual that grows and changes, a business model also changes in due course of time. The original solutions may look completely different form the current solution. Similarly, our startup went through such changes too.

Today, we are associated with several nationally recognised schemes. We are also implementing government projects pan-India.

Some of the stepping stones that I faced on the path of my career were the mixed feelings I received from my family and friends when I decided to start my own business. Adding to that, I liked a person who was from a different community, so convincing my family for our marriage was another challenge. After making several efforts to convince them, they finally accepted our relationship

After all these years and after all these struggles, when I see a dream of mine coming true, I feel nothing but gratitude for all the hard times that I have seen in my life. Those hard times that I went through bestowed upon me some new abilities: The ability to handle rejection, the ability to say ‘No’, and the ability to feel absolutely nothing.

Starting from leaving home for the first time, to starting my own business, to recovering from my depression, all the hardships in my life have made me aggressive, which has helped me bring out that 'will' in me, and work hard to achieve what I desire.

Hard things happen

To create more strength.

The more they occur,

The stronger you'll grow,

Higher will be the chances

And bigger will be the success.

Don't get scared by the stones that come in your way.

Thank all the tiny pebbles of life.

They are the catalysts playing a very vital role!

TO PRACTICE

- Write down all the hard times that you have faced in your past, and also mention the outcomes of those hardships that came about with due course of time. Pick the positive things and learning out of that.

- Write down the hard times that you are facing in the present, the current situation. Also mention what you hope the outcome to be. Focus on the outcome, stay positive and flow harmoniously with time.

The Path of Implication Of All Things Learnt

On this path, I implemented all the new things that I had learnt in my life to make it more balanced. This included:

- The Power of Mind
- Maintaining Emotional Quotient
- The Power of Writing
- The Power of Investing in the Self
- Qualities that made one a good leader, both in personal and professional life
- Understanding the difference between Pride and Confidence
- Power of Self-investment
- Adoption of Simplicity
- Understanding the importance of values

CHAPTER 7

LONG TERM SUSTAINABLE GRATIFICATION

Long-term gratification,

Is a by-product of Karma?

Karma involves our actions

Unfortunately, humans confuse Karma

With cultural and societal principles.

When we have to be in the system and perform all our duties and responsibilities accordingly, it becomes very important to understand that long-term gratification does not come by either stopping or searching for it. It comes with practice. We have to follow certain principles very rigorously to make it into a habit. There are certain points, which I observed during my journey:

- Follow your heart and soul's voice
- Do not mix your heart's voice with the societal rules

- Karma is something which needs to be taken care of all the time

- We should not mix-up our fears with karma

Long-term gratification is just another version of a powerful mind with strong emotions. The strength of emotions and sustainability of gratification should not depend on any of your habits. It means, we should practice certain doctrines till the time we are not dependent on anything.

Like what happened with me when I was walking this path, I got into the habit of writing. The day I write, I felt content, I like my environment, the people around me, and everything just looks and feels good to me. The practice of writing makes sure that my day goes perfectly fine. It is all unlike the days I do not get the time to write. Those days, I start getting frustrated quickly and nothing looks or feels good around me. It makes me reactive instead of proactive in life.

So, I worked more on understanding karma and the power of the mind, so that I do not get upset easily. Having stable emotions is very important as we are very much within the system, we have a family and kids to take care of. It is very much required to find a balance between things. While I have heard of people going in search of peace, I feel I am fortunate enough that I do not have to spend too much sweat in trying to search for it. Our peace basically lies in our families, and to stay in-tune with our hobbies. Only you can decide what makes you happy. No one else can or should decide it for you.

I had also realised that in order to get aligned with spiritually, I need to continuously practice and follow certain doctrines like a 'Yogi', because spirituality is something like a dope, an eternal dope. As a family person, one might not be able to follow it completely. However, there are several practices that can be followed to make it more sustainable. For instance, I started mitigating the reasons and causes behind my anger and hunger, since both of these are major factors that encourage impatience and intolerance in me. Yes, I am a Punjabi, but hunger here does not only mean my hunger for food. It can vary from my desire for money, for power, to be dominant, possessive, etc. All of these factors generate out of the inferiority complex or insecurity that we all have in our personalities.

In order to remove or control these negative traits in our personality, a person must not only be intelligent, but also emotionally strong. Having a good Emotional Intelligence/Quotient (EQ) is very much responsible in making a person self-sufficient. EQ also helps an individual enhance their learning skills, and become adaptive and flexible towards challenges. Using the emotional intelligence and cues provided to them in a certain situation, they are better able to formulate their behaviour and actions according to the situation. People with strong qualities and skill sets always find their way to work on their passions. Developing a strong EQ may take some time, but slowly and gradually as our EQ gets strong, we also become content.

While on the path of strengthening your personality, you will also get the opportunity to be bold on every front of your life. As I started working on my personality, slowly and gradually I gained the confidence to speak upfront on any issue or aspect of my life that I encountered. I got the confidence to put off all the baggage, which I used to be soaked in.

Either be silent or

Speak up

But

Don't prefer to be soaked in any case

This hobby turned habit of mine also helped to lightened up my mind. Now, I can think more and work more and maintain a perfect balance in my life.

The process of personality development requires one to be flexible. One needs to be flexible in terms of their mindset. One obstacle that almost everyone faces in their path is ego. Everyone has an ego. The intensity may vary, but ego plays a very important role in shaping our personality. This is why it is very important to keep a check on our ego. Usually, we misunderstand the overall meaning of the word ego itself.

Ego has always been perceived as a destructive trait of the personality. People talk very negatively about other people's high ego.

In a workplace, we see people who have a lofty ego and are not able to work in collaboration with their peers. Such people are low on empathy and emotional quotient. Over a span of time, such people become disappointed leaders.

Fundamentally, ego depicts one's personality in a dual manner. It is comprised of inferior complex/ jealousy and self-respect. The altitude of one's ego outlines the negative or positive version of a personality. This altitude also defines the level of one's emotional intelligence. EQ grows with practice and by adopting certain habits like reading, writing, learning something new, accepting others as they are, not expecting too much, etc. A study shows that people with a high EQ have a greater potential to become successful than people with a low EQ.

An organisation is defined by the qualities possessed by its leaders. Their personalities are reflected in almost all the processes that take place. This is because in an organisation, people tend to follow their leaders and emulate their behaviour and responses. You will be surprised to see the extent to which the personalities of the leaders in an organisation impact the personalities of its employees.

Sometimes, people with even good qualifications and a high IQ are not able to lead a team. This is where EQ stands apart from IQ and plays a vital role in giving a unique quality to the individual to function better in any formal or social space. (Some features of a good leader and a bad leader are mentioned in chapter 8).

TO PRACTICE

- Write down the situations in which your heart and mind are not aligned, and after a deep root analysis of the outcomes and everything, prefer to follow your heart in every situation. I am asking you to do this after a proper analysis of the situation because karma should always be taken care of prior to you taking your decisions.
- Measure the altitude of your ego, and check how many times in a day does it get hurt. If it gets hurt multiple times on a daily basis, start working on enhancing your knowledge base by exploring new things and terms in life.
- To balance your EQ, always be ready to learn new things out of all the small challenges that you face on a daily basis in life.

CHAPTER 8

MAKING OF A GOOD LEADER

Our mothers are our first teachers for all our skills. Since childhood, we are taught about different right and wrong doings. While we were kids, we have been scolded by our mothers some time or the other. These scoldings are life lessons, which only serve the purpose of teaching us how to become better human beings. Lessons like how to be compassionate, the value of money, and humility are some of the values, which are taught to us by our mothers during our formative years.

As a businesswoman, I have had quite some years of experience in the field of business. In all these years, I have met several people, but the one thing that has always bothered me is how to select the best leader to guide my team. I have met many people with a very high IQ, but they do not have the skillset to lead a team. This is what motivated and compelled me to write about the leadership qualities too.

While we were kids, our mothers always gave us the important life lessons from different situations in our lives. Quite often than not, most of us fall into the habit of pushing their advice to the back of our minds. My intention behind articulating some of the common traits of failed leaders is to provide similar advice, which all of us can relate to, and which is important to be known if one wants to build up a leadership personality. Before that, here is a list of behavioral signs observed in people who have poor leadership qualities:

1. **Lack of Integrity**

A true leader always keeps his or her word. Moral integrity not only defines a person amongst others, but also helps in building up the reputation of a company. Employees look up to their leaders to see what behaviour is actually acceptable. If a leader is involved in unethical behaviour, his or her employees will soon follow after too. A lack of moral integrity does, sooner or later, call for major troubles, which in turn leads to a person's undoing.

2. **Inability to cope with competition**

Great leaders know how to deal with problems in different situations by employing a range of leadership skills. There cannot be one solution to all the problems and great leaders know what approach to take in which situation. People with high EQ understand this simple truth and remain fluid. While a person with low EQ remains stuck in his or her ways due to their ego and their inability to cope with competition. 'My-way-or-the-highway' attitude is demonstrated by people with poor leadership qualities.

3. **Lack of or no future vision**

Few great business leaders have described a true leader as one whose job is to push forward, and whose vision is focused on making a better and a more productive future. More often than not, bad leaders often stay satisfied with the status quo. Progress cannot be expected from a leader who does not have a clear plan for how to continuously improve and progress.

4. **Cannot broaden his network in the corporate**

The best leaders know ways to broaden their horizon in the corporate. A good leader takes accountability for the mistakes of his company, and knows when to give credit to his employees. Employees look for such behaviour in the leader whom they are working for. People with low EQ are incapable of accepting their mistakes and deflect blame onto other people.

5. **No skill set to work in collaboration**

One of the most important traits for a leader is to have great communication skill. People with good communication skills are effectively able to communicate their plans and ideas to their employees. No matter how good the strategy is, if it is not communicated properly to the employees, it will never be successful. True leaders usually share their strategies with their employees in an easy to understand and motivational manner. Further, a good leader is also a good listener. If a person does not have the quality or the patience to listen, they will also not be able to deliver the required message. A leader effectively demonstrates his or her ideas and expectations to the employees.

Leadership is the key factor that ultimately leads a team to greatness. This is why a few factors must always be considered before you join a new team, or even hire a new member to your team.

There is no age limit to learning. Rather, once the learning stops, it hampers the growth of an individual at all levels. Anyone who wants to improve their skill set can learn these qualities mentioned below. These qualities are not new. We all have been taught about them in our childhood, or while we were growing up. Going through them now will help you interpret them in a new light. So, let us go back in our lives a little and remember what our parents have taught us, and practice them to ensure a healthy professional life.

1. **Knowledge is equal to freedom:**

Knowledge frees you from the darkness of ignorance. It is not simply limited to books. You can gain knowledge from your day-to-day activities and interactions with people whom you encounter or observe in life.

2. **Hard work always pays off**:

Most of us dwell in this insecurity that we might lose all our hard earned money one day. If a leader does not have faith in his work, troubles will come knocking at his door sooner or later.

3. **Take some time out for devotion**:

Many of us may not get the time to visit the temple every day, but we must try to take some time out to sit and pray. Prayer helps in relieving your anxiety and stress, and gives clarity to your mind. After all, the divine creator is truly the only one who can help us out with our messy lives and times of misery!

4. **Be humble**:

Humility is an important feature of the character of a true leader. The market comes with its ups and downs. Thus, we must never be arrogant about money or career.

5. **Always look your best**:

While many of us (someone like me particularly) do like dressing up, there are people who find this to be a tedious job.

6. **Dress up!**

Dressing up is important in business because you never know when you will meet someone important; you definitely want to leave a good impression on them.

7. **Try new things in life:**

Whenever you get the chance, try out new things in life, like learning a new skill, reading a new book, trying out a new sport, making a new investment, designing, etc. You don't necessarily have to be an expert to participate in it, but you must keep saying yes to every opportunity that comes your way.

8. **Read new books:**

They are the best means of self-education. Books help us gather wisdom from the generations of writers who have existed before us. When we read new books, we gain new insights and outlook on life.

9. **Health is wealth:**

Always, as all our mothers say, we must keep our health and happiness at the top priority. Take time out for yourself. You can either do exercise, yoga, or indulge in some self-pampering, like going out shopping, etc. Do anything that makes you happy. It is important to understand that the key to a blissful life is knowing your needs first.

10. **Prioritise love and joy over materialistic things:**

We all know that money is important, but we must be able to assign the right amount of value to it in our life. Overindulgence in materialistic things will only make us dependent on it.

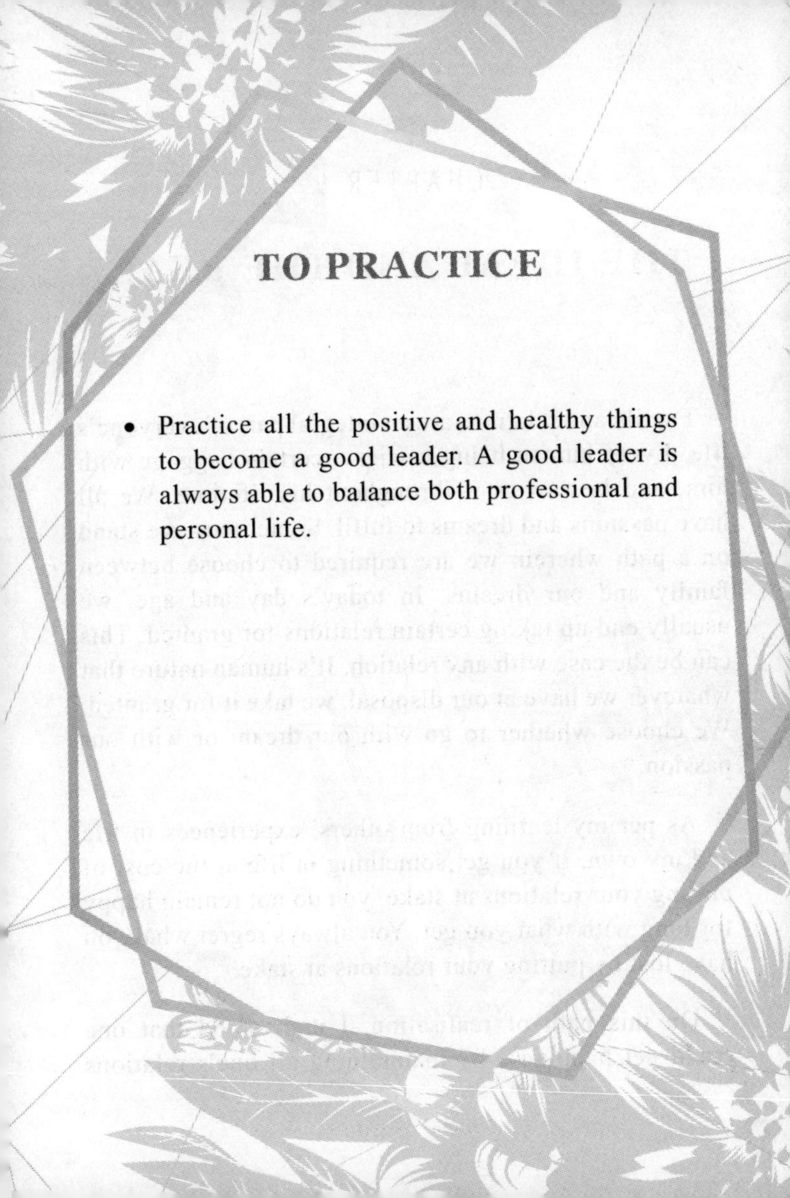

TO PRACTICE

- Practice all the positive and healthy things to become a good leader. A good leader is always able to balance both professional and personal life.

CHAPTER 9

THE IDEAL AND THE REAL

Family and relations are an integral part of everyone's life. Every human being carries a certain baggage with him, and he carries it throughout his lifetime. We all have passions and dreams to fulfil. Sometimes, we stand on a path wherein we are required to choose between family and our dreams. In today's day and age, we usually end up taking certain relations for granted. This can be the case with any relation. It's human nature that whatever we have at our disposal, we take it for granted. We choose whether to go with our dream or with our passion.

As per my learning from others' experiences in life and my own, if you get something in life at the cost of putting your relations at stake, you do not remain happy for long with what you get. You always regret what you have lost by putting your relations at stake.

On this path of realisation, I understood that one could get happiness by maintaining all one's relations in a balance. Sometimes, we need to spend some little time and energy into keeping our relations healthy and balanced. They must not be taken for granted.

Healthy and satisfactory happiness lies in the completion of your dreams while keeping your relations balanced. Over a span of time, while you work on your passion, you will figure out ways to balance the relations in your life and will see the results at the same time. This will boost up your morale too because of your balanced work and life relations.

The term 'real' refers to something, which is a fact, or something that is permanent. The term 'ideal' refers to something, which is convenient. While on one hand, 'real' is related to 'what is', 'ideal' is bothered with 'what ought to be'. Similarly, there are real family goals and ideal family goals. Real family goals are the ones that are achievable, while the ideal family goals are the ones, which a family is supposed to achieve. In order to have a happy and peaceful family life, it is very important to understand the difference between the 'ideal' and the 'real'. No matter what your position or salary is, what is the point of earning so much money if you cannot spend it on your loved ones.

One of the major supporting factors in the lives of successful people is their family. There is huge sacrifice in a human's life to retain it. It is the family that helps us differentiate between the ideal and the real things in the world.

I myself have seen the failures of people who could not remain with their families, and failed to achieve that balance and harmony in life. My grandmother was from Lahore. Being a refugee in India after partition, my grandfather had to do a lot of hard work in his life, and hence my father did so too. My father was in another country when my grandfather died. I can deeply feel those moments that my father always remembered. He regretted only one thing, which was not being able to make it to his father's funeral. I was very close to my father and had a very clear idea that my family is something for which I can't find any substitute in my life. My father died in 2016 and at that time, I did all his rituals and rites on my own. When I came back from my father's funeral rituals, my life transitioned from one phase to another. I got everything that a normal person desires in one's life. Every single wish of mine got realised within a year of my father's death. Today, I feel my father's soul with me, as an angel showering blessings on my life.

TO PRACTICE

Try to retain relations and family till your last effort, this is a lifetime success if one is able to breakthrough it.

CHAPTER 10

PRIDE AND CONFIDENCE

After eight long years, the business that my husband and I started from scratch has become what we may call a 'family business'. It was our vision from the very beginning that for all the key positions in the company, we will always choose our own family members. Initially, things were good. Over a span of time, things started changing slowly and gradually. I was at the front window of the company. I was the spokesperson who got involved in all the meetings with government officials and corporate clients. Due to this exposure, the horizon of my thoughts expanded exponentially, and I learnt a lot of professional etiquettes as time moved on. But the one odd thing that I found myself dealing with was that my key people, basically my colleagues who were handling backend, did not get much chance or opportunity to gain such an exposure, and their thought processes remained the same as before.

Now when our thought processes started to grow out of sync, I had to handle my colleagues with that leap. I felt it as a big challenge in my life, as both my personal and professional interests were attached to those people who were in key positions at the company. What I wanted from them professionally, I started asking them for it with confidence, but they started taking it as my pride. My expectation of perfection in the job was perceived as my pride.

Seeking perfection

Is not

Being arrogant.

This challenge made me understand that there is a very thin line between pride and confidence. People filled with utmost confidence often seem to be very proud. Mostly, confident people carry with them an attitude, which is their lifestyle. If one continuously practices to carry this style, it eventually becomes one's lifestyle later on. Confidence can come from various factors like power, wealth, intelligence, and many other capabilities.

It is a lifetime's project to maintain and carry this lifestyle. This needs practice, learning new things, becoming independent, moving more and more towards the achievement of one's goals in life, meeting new people, reading good books, having a good network and many more things which make one a confident individual.

For them, it was a new learning because they had to learn how to become more confident from the beginning. This is the million-dollar question. As I have mentioned before, there are two types of quotients in a human being, i.e., IQ and EQ. People born with a higher IQ are always confident and strong enough to maintain their lifestyle as they want. On the other side, there are people who do not carry a high IQ, but have a high EQ. With a high EQ, an individual can gain confidence by learning new things and adopting a positive attitude.

The first step to acquire confidence is to overcome the fear of life and get a new purpose to live your life. The incorporation of an inferiority complex can be the result of various things, like your upbringing, your societal influence, networking, etc. It is not so easy to overcome your fear, but it is also not an impossible task. Your confidence can rise higher than even your EQ.

Once one practices EQ, she or he starts observing and understanding people however they are. One identifies more reliable ways to attract confidence. While practicing, one must remain silent and receive more power to overcome fear.

So, I am always pleased to say, “My attitude is my confidence, and it’s my lifestyle!

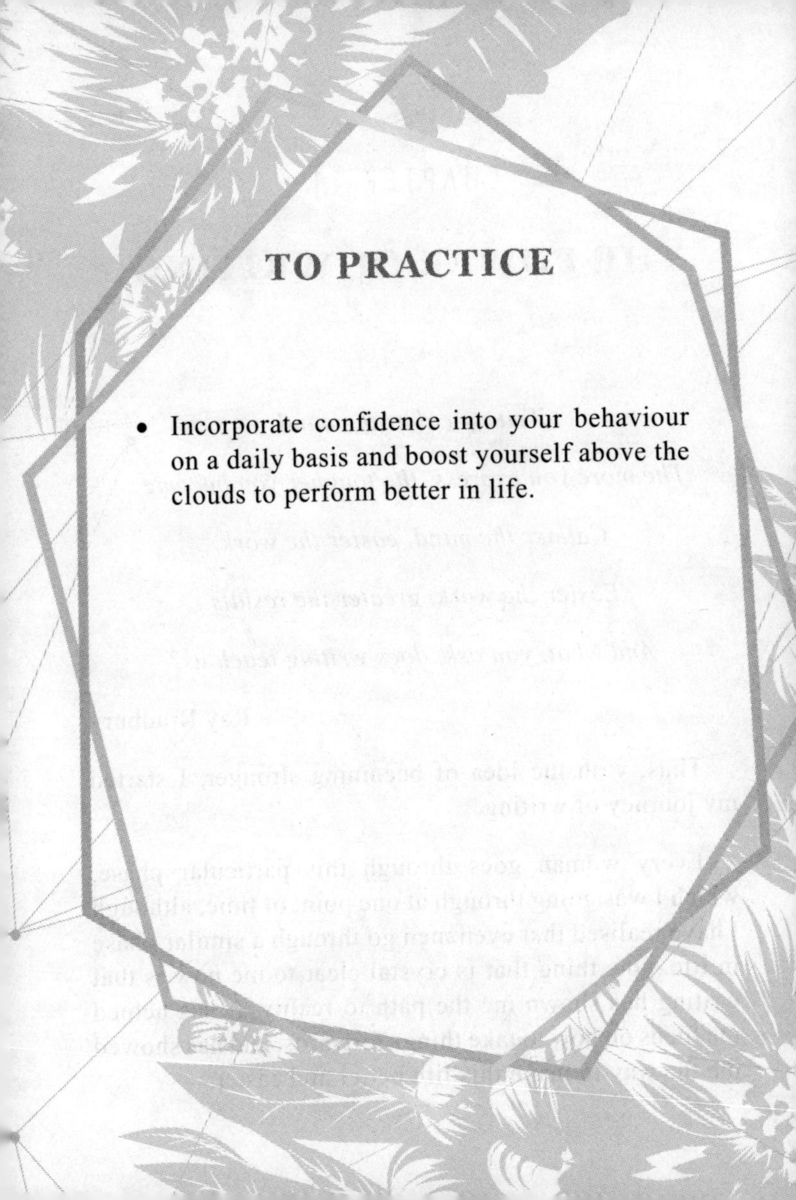

TO PRACTICE

- Incorporate confidence into your behaviour on a daily basis and boost yourself above the clouds to perform better in life.

CHAPTER 11

THE POWER OF WRITING

Writing calms the mind,

The more you express, the tougher you become,

Calmer the mind, easier the work,

Easier the work, greater the results.

And what, you ask, does writing teach us?

~ Ray Bradbury

Thus, with the idea of becoming stronger, I started my journey of writing.

Every woman goes through this particular phase, which I was going through at one point of time, although I have realised that even men go through a similar phase in life. One thing that is crystal clear to me now is that writing has shown me the path to reality. It has helped me focus on how to take things forwards, and has showed me the way to make this life better and easier.

So, there is this thing, as I was preparing myself to become stronger, I was getting even stronger vibes to achieve it. This feeling itself was strong enough to calm me down and has eventually helped me to soar above my weak EQ. My personality reformed as I started writing. Writing makes me feel like I am gradually getting victory over my fears.

Started writing

Strengthened my mind,

Toughened my emotions,

I feel no panic,

Leading myself to a new world

And

That is Victory.

The most important things that I have learnt with writing and for which I am really thankful are:

- Writing has helped me find my inner true self
- Writing gave me the confidence to explore my inner feelings, and showed me how to be at peace with them
- Writing made me realise the value of people, especially those who are different from me

- Writing forced me to ask questions about what is important in life
- Writing taught me to take risk in my life
- Writing taught me to feel, rather than just looking at the world through the lens of science
- Writing helped me maintain my family relations
- Writing helped me find God again

This is how I entered into the second part of this path, and I am still walking on this path. I have named this chapter, 'The path to finding the inner self by strengthening emotions over fear'.

A normal human being lives a monotonous life which includes going to the office, doing some workout, sitting for a little chit-chat with the colleagues, household work, spending time with the family members and so on. Almost every day ends up like this unless something extraordinary takes place. About a year back, I was also leading the same monotonous life. Being into the system at a both personal and professional front, we all have several complaints from our lives and we discuss about these things many times with our friends and colleagues whom we feel close to.

I started articulating all my emotions through writing. I progressed and witnessed a strong change in my personality over a span of time, and this change made me emotionally stronger.

With the help of writing, I am now able to handle all my emotions and distance myself from the petty issues, which do not play any significant role in my life, but only exist to always create a ruckus. Subsequently, after devoting a complete year in trying to write professionally, my whole personality changed.

I experienced a few of the following wonderful changes. I could:

- Clearly set my goals in life
- Identify the purpose of my life
- Handle the issues of daily life
- Balance both personal and professional life

One of the biggest changes I experienced was that I became 'a completely non-judgmental person'. I found peace and solace in writing, and whenever I see other people judging or giving their comments over something now, I feel like escaping from those conversations and ignoring their judgments.

I find topics from my daily life to write on, and am successfully living a balanced life now with no complaints or regrets.

Everyone has some hobby or the other. You may like singing, dancing, drawing, etc. I will strongly suggest for everyone to practice what they like best at least once every day. You will see the magic (in the form of personality changes) transforming your life too.

TO PRACTICE

Try to pen down all those emotions, which you do not expect yourself to express. Practice it till you are able to express them. Once you express them, there shall be no one else braver or bolder than you.

CHAPTER 12

THE POWER OF INVESTING IN THE SELF

Out of all the lessons that I have learnt during my career, this is the most important *gyan* that I would like to share with everyone. Investing on yourself, firstly, does not mean self-indulgence or self-spoiling; it means that you are devoted to yourself first, which is the fundamental way of carrying on a healthy lifestyle.

We don't understand our self-worth until the ground beneath our feet shakes. We don't understand that we are giving up some great opportunities that an enhanced energy, active presence and confidence can give us!

What is self-investment?

It means being devoted to yourself in order to enhance your intellect, knowledge base, power, and confidence to upgrade the worth of your individuality. This devotion can be practiced in any form, like joining a new course, a workshop, attending guest lectures, learning new terms, reading new books, and many more likewise. Every individual is born with an immense potential. It is thus the responsibility of each one of us to develop our gifts and talents, whether by developing our existing skills or by learning new ones, developing ourselves personally or professionally, or by tapping into our creativity, etc. We need to serve ourselves first, before we work or act to serve the others.

While there are numerous benefits to self-investment, for me, the one reason why it is important is because it gives a clear message to the other people that my values and potential are important for me, and that I am going to invest in it enough time, space and energy that is important for me to grow.

Some of the benefits that come with self-investment are:

1) No tension for retirement:

When we invest in ourselves—whether it's through learning something new or by refining our existing skills, we help ourselves add more value to our lives. Not only does skill development ensure a stable future, our skills stay with us throughout our lifetime. A person with skills does not retire. In fact, with regular self-investment, they grow even more after retirement due to more values.

2) Becoming independent:

Saying yes to self-investment—whether by enrolling for a workshop, going for a checkup, or for mountain hiking, and so on—can boost not only your confidence tremendously, but also make you feel more independent. When you have confidence and independence, you can achieve more things than you would ever have thought possible. You will be able to set your goals higher, and also reach those goals that you once thought were out of your reach.

3) Become a Brand in yourself:

Investing in oneself also means spending more time with likeminded people. This will give you the opportunity to forge new connections and make useful friends. The wider your connections, more will be your value. When you have connections on a large scale, you become a brand.

4) Peace of Mind:

Many a times, we avoid investing in ourselves because we feel that we are not worth it, either due to the lack of time or finances, or we simply pass on the opportunity by telling ourselves that we will do it someday. But trust me, when you take out the time to invest in yourself, the sense of accomplishment and satisfaction you get in return is tremendous. You can choose to invest in fitness, health, or creative pursuits, but once you achieve or finish something, the accomplishment can be extremely beneficial and can do wonders for your mindset and attitude.

After reading this chapter, ask yourself this question, 'Do I want to try something new or learn something new for myself?'

If the answer is yes, just go for it! Don't hold back! You will definitely see the benefits either immediately or as future rewards.

Investing in yourself will enhance your worth; you are your own asset.

How to invest in yourself?

- Read a good book
- Learn a new language
- Explore the new futuristic technology
- Meet good and intellectual people
- Join online courses to enhance your knowledge base

It is always worth investing in yourself other than bonds, stocks or properties.

Invest in yourself as much as you can.

You are your own biggest asset by far.

~ Warren Buffet

CHAPTER 13

SIMPLE LIVING, HIGH THINKING

When you want something, all the universe conspires in helping you to achieve it

~ Paulo Coelho

My journey on this path is still underway and is far from being over. Every day, I learn new things. After understanding the power of materialism, fears and anxieties over my mind, I started exploring the miraculous hidden powers of the mind. This power was already always there in my mind. This power is the power to 'change'. Change can be of various types. While some changes have the capacity to bring in immense benefits, there are certain changes on the other hand, which have the power to destroy what you already have. Following the realisations, the changes that I made in my life have not only proved to be beneficial for me, but also for the people around me. This power to 'change' is already hidden in all of us. We just need to explore it by breaking the shackles around our minds.

Slavery and ecstasy cannot walk together,

Either be elated, or be a slave.

When one is on the path of overcoming one's fears, one gains the ability to evaluate even the tiniest of things.

After realising the power of materialistic things over me, I started changing and my mood started getting better. I gradually started understanding the real meaning of life too.

We, as youngsters, tend to forget what our parents teach us. We believe in our experience, rather than gaining from their wisdom. As I started understanding the true meaning of life, I started realising why my father had been so restrictive? Why he had always stopped me from falling in love with artificial things. He always stopped me from doing all those tasks which involved being fake. Trust me, being fake is time-consuming too.

He always advised me to remain simple, even when I was studying in school. At that time, I was only a child, unknown of the 'realities' of life, or whatever you may like calling it. At that time, I did not, in fact, could not understand that consuming artificial things would only make me more and more dependent on those things, and with due course of time, I would find myself in the clutches of materialistic things. I did not know that it would boil my life down to satisfy all those requirements.

This meant, I would be away from the far bigger and more important intellectual things.

I lost my father two and a half years back, but he had been guided me with his wisdom for two decades before that. Today, as I understand the underlying meaning of all that he said, I have realised how much he was aware about the true meaning of life. Now my son is only four years old, and I know that he will probably not understand everything that I tell him, but yes, a day will come even in his life when he will realise the underlying depth of my advices. I consider all those learnings that I received from my father as my values. These are the values, which are my foundation, and I consider one's values as the map for one's destination of leading a balanced life. The author of the famous book *Seven Habits of Highly Effective People* has explained it very beautifully by taking the analogy of a map and destination.

What will happen if you get the wrong map for your destination? You will be irritated, you will be frustrated, and your attitude and behavior will be pathetic, as you will not be able to reach your destination in time or through the correct way. On the other hand, you will happily reach your destination, and in the right time too, as long as you have the right map with you. Similarly, I feel that my father's advices are my values, and those values create the map for me to reach my destination, which is the attainment of a balanced life with the blessings of God in my family. I have incorporated his advices into my habits today to walk the right path for the rest of my life.

Adoption of simplicity with one's own consent

Is a freedom

Forcible incorporation of it

Is a prison.

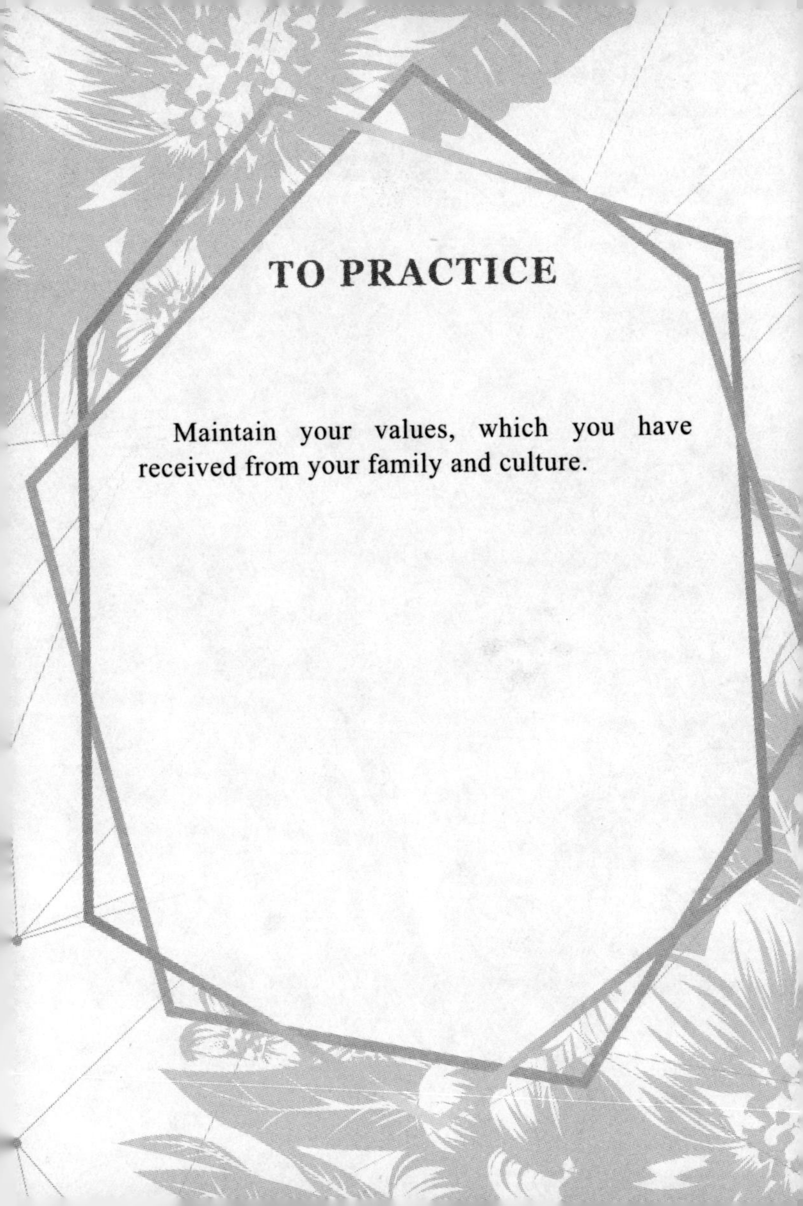

TO PRACTICE

Maintain your values, which you have received from your family and culture.

AUTHOR'S NOTE

My strength and self-motivation were the only two elements of my personality that kept me going. I kept motivating myself to keep my aim high and create my own path to success.

In this book, I have penned down all my experiences, and it would bring me immense happiness if even a single thought from this book is able to contribute and bring even 1 per cent of positivity in a reader's life. My opinions and views are entirely based on my personal experiences and can be subjective, but I have tried my best to put forward the most logical inferences.

Thank you for reading this book. You can learn more about my journey by following my LinkedIn and Facebook account. Follow #preetspeaks

ABOUT THE AUTHOR

Preet Sandhu is a naturally enthusiastic, result-oriented professional with more than ten years of experience and interest in 'Skill Services', that includes but is not limited to operations, stakeholder management, administration and project management.

At present, she is the Chief Operating Officer of All India Technical Management Council and is leading a team of more than hundred employees.

She is the active Executive Director of AITMC Ventures Pvt. Ltd. and the founder of Model Career Centre under AITMC. AITMC-MCC was formed with the signing of an MoU with the Ministry of Labour and Employment in the 6th AITMC Annual Summit in 2017. AITMC-MCC helps linking the youth (job seekers) with jobs and career-related

She also wrote several articles for various magazines like Business World and TSSC's annual magazine, *Telco Times*.